AF368468

HER

GLIMPSES

Alethea Phoebe Nongrum

BookLeaf Publishing

India | USA | UK

Copyright © Alethea Phoebe Nongrum
All Rights Reserved.

This book has been self-published with all reasonable efforts taken to make the material error-free by the author. No part of this book shall be used, reproduced in any manner whatsoever without written permission from the author, except in the case of brief quotations embodied in critical articles and reviews.

The Author of this book is solely responsible and liable for its content including but not limited to the views, representations, descriptions, statements, information, opinions, and references ["Content"]. The Content of this book shall not constitute or be construed or deemed to reflect the opinion or expression of the Publisher or Editor. Neither the Publisher nor Editor endorse or approve the Content of this book or guarantee the reliability, accuracy, or completeness of the Content published herein and do not make any representations or warranties of any kind, express or implied, including but not limited to the implied warranties of merchantability, fitness for a particular purpose.

The Publisher and Editor shall not be liable whatsoever...

Made with ❤ on the BookLeaf Publishing Platform

www.bookleafpub.in

www.bookleafpub.com

Dedication

To that shy *little girl* who dared to dream and aim for the stars;
And to my best friend, my darling *mother*.

Preface

HER: GLIMPSES, is a small collection of poems
that I had written in the course of twenty one
days for the *"twenty-one day challenge"*
organised by The Book Leaf Publishing.
The poems do not follow any particular
theme, but they mostly revolve around my
life- there are glimpses from my childhood,
some from my teen days and some from the
present. There are also poems that are **NOT**
based on my life but rather, they are prompts
that came to mind during the challenge and
by penning them down, they turned to
glimpses of my thoughts.

Acknowledgements

My deepest gratitude goes to **Book Leaf Publishing**, who through its twenty one day challenge- #TheWriteAngle, has given newbie writers like me an opportunity to share our art with others and a chance to be published. Through this challenge, not only have I been forced to step out of my comfort zone, but I have also been able to look at the world around me with different and newer perspectives, helping me improve day by day and become more confident.

I would also like to thank my pillar of strength, my dearest **Mother**, for always backing me and my sometimes crazy plans. You are my safe place, my best friend and the one who I can always run to. Thank you for being the coolest and best mom ever.

And last but not least, thank you to all the **readers** who chose to give this book a try. I know that it is far from perfect and it might be a little all over the place, but I hope you can look past that and forgive my inexperience.

Thank you to all once again.
Happy Reading!

1. To Her

To *her* for whom the sky held so much wonder-
A passing cloud, a twinkling star,
Each with their own story to tell.
The sun a guiding light, the moon a friend by night,
Pure joy she felt from oh so little.

To *her* for whom the green fields were pure beauty-
Dew drops on a blade of grass, petrichor in the air;
A sense of content on a summer day.
Wildflowers, butterflies and bush berries,
They had never, nor will they ever make her gray.

To *her* for whom living life was so simple-
When winning meant an empty bowl of rice,
Or just simply being told you were nice.
When anything was possible if you were a little older;
That was when *her* life was clearer.

To *her* for whom faith in *her* dreams could make them
come true;
Go for it dear!
For even if no one does, I'll always believe in *you.*

2. Magic Days

Bumps and bruises on their knees,
Chasing dragonflies,fleeing from bees.
Jumping rope and dodging balls,
Climbing trees, not afraid of a fall.

Trading cards and collecting marbles,
Sometimes even playful squabbles.
Making house and dumb charades,
Not a single worry for our grades.

Weekends were the magic days,
To play till sunset we'd find our ways.
Faces plastered with gleeful smiles,
Everything then was all worthwhile.
Oh those precious days of then!
Even now are still golden.

3. True Love

Like the morning sunshine, she adds warmth to your
day,
Like the north star, she shines to lead you on your way;
Like the cool gentle breeze that tempers the hot summer,
If she's beside you, everything just gets a little better.

When the world beats you down and you've about given
up,
A shoulder she'll lend and much more for her pup;
When failure's all you see and you're too tired to try,
That's when she'll say, *"You've done well my love, let it
out in a cry."*

There's nothing you can do that can take away her love,
You're the apple of her eye, no one stands above.
I hope you'll always remember her love is like no other,
For it is a precious love, the love of a **Mother.**

4. Tough Love

She stands firm- her shoulders back with her head held
high,
To win and to conquer, she will give it her all;
Her wings she spreads as she soars to the sky,
Those little fears and doubts will never make her fall.
Small steps at a time till she reaches the top,
Her body wants to quit but her mind cheers her still;
Until her dreams are realized she will never stop,
Her heart's deepest desires she will one day fulfill.

When she makes up her mind to pave her own way,
She will march on forward, there's no turning back;
There's nothing you can say to make her will sway,
All because self worth and confidence she does not lack.
She learned to adapt to all kinds of weather,
She learned all this by looking up to her **Father.**

5. Louie

The *wagging of her tail* the moment she senses I'm near,
The hope and trust she has in me, in her eyes so clear;
It's her little excited jumps when she's extra happy,
It's her running around in circles ever so freely-
It's the little things she does that makes loving her so
easy.

Her *little playful barks*, a sweet music to my ear,
Her love and affection for me I'd always hold dear;
The paw that she would put on my lap whenever I'm
low,
The sweet smile just to make me laugh, she knows just
when to show-
How can so much love from a little pup overflow?

There's just so much love when it comes to her,
But there's one thing I hate, my biggest fear;

I fear that one day, her with her brown fur I'd no longer
see,
That one day, just a distant memory she will be-
Oh how I hope that day would never come, my precious
Louie.

6. Rain

With the dark clouds hovering over and everything
looking gray,
You peek out from your window and it seems to be a bad
day;
Soon enough you hear the tapping sounds on your
window pane,
Well it seems like it's already started, *here comes the
rain;*
The air turns cold and suddenly it feels almost gloomy-
You start to miss the warm days, the days when it was
sunny.

As the clock ticks, the pouring rain only gets louder,
So you might just as well tune it out, make yourself
comfier-
With a warm cup of tea and a blanket wrapped snugly
around you,

Still that heavy and uneasy feeling you can't get used to;
It's that feeling of the blues that just looms in the air,
You try your best to be indifferent but it's just glaringly
there.

The rain often times feels depressing and like a burden,
But growing up I've realised one thing for certain;
Though it might bring some hassle and dampen the
weather,
It refreshes and brings out a unique calm in nature;
And soon after you'll see that all things are well and fine,
You'll come to see that *after the darkest times comes the
brightest sunshine.*

7. The Route

A narrow winding route bounded by picturesque hills
and mountains;
In the green and lush summer, the fog covers everything
in white,
Making you feel like you're swimming in the clouds up
in heaven.
The sound of the waterfalls formed by the summer rain;
The rich earthy scent of the wet soil and the fresh scent
of the trees,
They make you feel serene as they make you forget your
pain.

In the cold and dry winter, the route is bound to tell a
different story;
You say, *"See you next summer,"* to the fog as you greet
the beautiful deep canyons,
And even as the green fades to yellow, the route loses
not its glory.

There's sunshine abundant and with it the beautiful blue
sky;
The chilly breeze blows over the now dry grass making
them sway,
It makes you feel a sense of longing and you don't know
why.

So now you know the route in summer and in winter,
A route always perfect no matter the weather;
A route that brings peace and joy no matter where you
roam,
Well that is the route to where everything started-
The route Home.

8. Jewels Of My Crown

One is my **purple**-
Always strong yet still so gentle.
Then there is my **blue**-
The one I can always run to.
Another's my **red**-
Love and kindness is what she spreads.
Followed by my **yellow**-
She's one whose words I always follow.
Also there's my **white**-
Her soul and mind so pure and bright.
And then there's my **black**-
The girl who always has my back.

9. Fire

She frowns as she stares at the reflection in the mirror;
Blank and weary eyes staring back at her,
The dark eye bags not making them any better.
The passion and fire no longer there,
The duller they look, the harder she stares.

She blinks and the reflection morphs into someone
younger,
Her sixteen year old self right before her;
Her eyes so vibrant and full of life, a whole lot brighter.
Those young eyes bore into the eyes much older,
Wanting to revive them once more, itching to inspire.

In those young eyes she saw both the *dreamer* and the
fighter,
She saw the little girl who never stopped aiming higher-
The girl who pushed herself up even if she fell ten times
harder.

The determination she had reflected in her eyes so clear,
She never did quit, she swallowed her fears.

Another blink and the sixteen year old girl was no
longer there,
She smiles blissfully as she senses a change in the air;
It took one look into her eyes- there's no more despair.
There's a *new flame* that's starting to ignite within her,
She can feel it deep down in her heart, she's got back the
Fire.

10. Human

Why are you so polite if she's pretty?
And so charming if he comes from money?
You respect them if they have a Master's degree,
And if they know someone wealthy,
Why are you suddenly all friendly?

But change the scene, make her *"ugly"*,
Then I bet all the good manners from you flee.
Your ego soars high the moment you see-
Someone who's not doing as well as *"thee"*,
Someone who struggles for every penny.

What a world we live in, what a cruel society!
There's neither love nor kindness, nor is there empathy.
Tolerance and honour- only for the high and mighty,
While to the ones who live in poverty-
You strip them of everything, even their dignity.

Why must we be so hideous and unkind?
Nothing but seeds of contempt we sow,
Yet we think that everything's fine.
Well it's not, and it'll just get worse with time,
Being *"human"*, now merely just a paradigm.

11. Little Things

It's the **little things** in life-
That *sweet smile* from a stranger,
Or that *small wave* from your neighbour;
That little *thank you* that's said,
Or that *gentle pat* on your head;
Those *heartfelt words* of affirmation,
Or simply how they pay *attention*;
That *shoulder* you lean on,
Or that freshly formed *bond*;
The little *pushes* to make you better,
Or the *bad jokes* that still earn your laughter;
The *hugs* that make all your sadness shed,
Or the *hands* that always keep you fed;
Those small *achievements* that deserve much celebration,
Or those precious *tears* of determination;
That beautiful *pink sky* right at the break of dawn,
Or the *singing* of the birds in the morn;
It's these **little things** that make us feel alive.

12. Enough

You ask her to smile and to laugh,
But when she does, she's obnoxious.
You say beauty is what's on the inside,
But behind her back, you say *"pretty"* is what she lacks.

You say she can dress however she likes,
But she wears a mini skirt, and you push her to the dirt.
You ask her to be louder, a little bit braver,
But when she raises her voice, you claim it's just some
irksome noise.

You tell her she can be whoever she wishes to be,
But a *CEO*? No! That'll just hurt your ego.
You tell her she can climb higher up the ladder,
But the moment she gets too close to the top, you put in
extra effort to make her stop.

What is with you and your paradox?
Why do you want to trap her in your small box?

Has she not suffered too long with a life so tough?
Has she not gone through more than **enough**?

13. Youth

As *fresh* as the leaves in the summer,
As *colourful* as the blooming flowers;
As *gentle* yet as *persistent* as a river,
An *untamed soul* that never wavers.

The time when dreams flood your mind,
The *purpose of life-* you try to find;
The burning passion you can't confine,
Fear and doubt you leave behind.

When life's all about the experiences,
Whether rain showered, or sun kissed;
When it doesn't matter if you swing and miss,
To me, that's what **youth** is.

14. The Rose

It starts as a small unopened bud,
Engulfed by the sepals, *protected and loved.*
The warmth and light from the sunshine it craves,
But also the cool, light showers of the rain it awaits.
A little shy to fully unfurl its beautiful petals,
Hiding them for a bit more, yes only a little.
At just the right time the bright red colour bursts forth,
Its beauty unparalleled, thers's no match on earth.

But as the rule of the world reads: *no beauty left
untouched,*
Leave it to man to always follow through as such.
Though thorns it grew to keep it safe,
I bet a man still can't behave.
The bright red not as bright as before,
With some of its petals now rotten on the floor.
What of its life? What of its beauty?
It stood no chance against **hearts so ugly.**

15. Queen

Now the *little girl's all grown up,*
New responsibilities fill her cup;
Her sweet childhood gone too soon,
It might be a bane or it could be a boon.

There's no more unpredictable fun,
Instead there are *duties to be done*;
The role of being a good woman rests on her shoulders,
To be an example for all the younger daughters.

The older she gets, the more that she knows-
There are a lot of things that other people impose;
But still she smiles though *her heart cries,*
Maybe the life she's living is full of lies.

Still she carries on without a frown,
And she proudly wears her crown;
For no matter what storms come her way,
She'll come out a **winner** at the end of the day.

16. Home

Blessed to have a *roof over my head*,
Blessed to have a *comfortable bed*,
Surrounded by the *safety of four walls;*
But to me, that's not what home is;
For home is not only a place you live in,
But its a place of *comfort and meaning-*
A place you can *freely be yourself* in.

Home is in a *mother's warm embrace*,
It's in the *smile* of a loved one's face;
Home is where you *laugh without fear*,
Where for your *success* they cheer;
Home is what your **heart holds dear.**

17. Strong

You say a woman is strong when-
She knows how to say no,
And she's not just some show.
You say a woman is strong when-
She expects nothing less than respect,
And never leave her words unsaid.
You say a woman is strong when-
She stands on her own two feet,
And she never accepts defeat.
You say a woman is strong when-
She opens her own doors,
And always settles her scores.

But a woman is also strong when-
She's kind, soft and gentle,
And even if she chooses to settle.
A woman is strong when-
Silence becomes her only choice
To protect herself from all the chaos.

A woman is strong when-
Home-making is her thing,
Along with caring and nurturing.
A woman is also strong when-
She wants to cry out for help,
When she cannot seem to save herself.

A woman is strong not because of what she is,
Or what she can be;
She is strong simply because **she's a woman.**

18. Gemini

In the depths of her soul, there's a *fire* ablaze;
Yet like a cool *spring breeze*, there's a calmness on her
face.
Her thoughts rage like the mighty *turbulent waves*,
Yet only a quiet *stillness* her body portrays.

To others she *smiles* as bright as the sun,
While on the inside she *cries*, she wants it all to be done.
She brings them laughter, joy and a whole lot of fun,
While to herself, though she tries there's always none.

Her wings she spreads to *soar* up high,
But soon she clips them, she's *scared* to fly.
And now she wonders as time goes by,
If she'll always live a life of contradictions-
for after all she's a ***Gemini***.

19. The Cheeriest Girl

A smile here, a laugh there,
Oh how cheerful she is.
An *"It's okay,"* here, an *"I'll be fine,"* there,
Is that what kindness is?

A win here, a triumph there,
She holds her head up high.
The whole world looks up to her,
Can she dare to let out a sigh?

Always perfect, always right,
Always strong and ready to fight.
No flaw, no doubt or ripple,
But what if she's a liitle brittle?

For behind it all, behind that tough wall,
A girl sits frightened, wondering if she'll fall.
Diamonds on her cheeks a sharp contrast to the night,
And yet can no one see her plight?

In just a blink she might crumble,
Her whole world might be in shambles.
But no, her mind cannot be in a whirl,
Why? Because she's the *"cheeriest girl"*.

20. Path

She took a step and held her breath,
That was it, she'd make her bet.
Too young to know any better,
Did they know what's right for her?
They made her walk 'fore she changed her mind,
All alone, with no one behind.

The further she walked it only got harder,
Nothing but darkness all around her.
Everything was silent, almost dead,
Save for the *voices* in her head-
That were getting too real and loud,
Filling her with nothing but doubt.

She took a little glimpse around,
Only one thing of meaning she found-
A pretty little white *flower*,
That made the dark night a bit brighter.
Then it dawned on her,

She was her life's own *author.*

Like the flower that still bloomed in the dark,
She too was determined to make her mark.
Though she might be a little lost,
She'll find her way back, she'll run her own course.
She'll reach for her dreams and she won't look back,
Because now she's making her **own path**.

21. Dear Self

Dear self, here's my wish for you-
To be strong and to stand your ground,
To never be pushed around;
To be brave and face your fears,
Even if you shed some tears;
To always aim and dream high,
To know your limit is the sky;
To be kind though at times it may be hard,
To love and care with all your heart;
To yourself to always be true,
And never ever forget to **love you**.

www.ingramcontent.com/pod-product-compliance
Lightning Source LLC
LaVergne TN
LVHW010022200726
843495LV00015B/1876